Stardust
to
Soul
Speak

UNCOVERING MESSAGES
FROM THE UNIVERSE THAT
WERE MEANT FOR YOU

Erin Whitten

**THOUGHT
CATALOG**
Books

THOUGHTCATALOG.COM

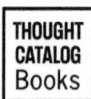

THOUGHT CATALOG Books

Copyright © 2025 Erin Whitten.

All rights reserved. No part of this book may be reproduced or transmitted in any form or any means, electronic or mechanical, without prior written consent and permission from Thought Catalog.

Published by Thought Catalog Books, an imprint of Thought Catalog, a digital magazine owned and operated by The Thought & Expression Co. Inc., an independent media organization founded in 2010 and based in the United States of America. For stocking inquiries, contact stockists@shopcatalog.com.

Produced by Chris Lavergne and Noelle Beams
Art direction and design by KJ Parish
Circulation management by Isidoros Karamitopoulos

thoughtcatalog.com | shopcatalog.com

First Edition, Limited Edition Print
Printed in select countries by Amazon.com.

ISBN 978-1-965820-02-5

Table of Contents

ZODIAC WHISPERS   11

Aries   13
Taurus   17
Gemini   21
Cancer   25
Leo   29
Virgo   33
Libra   37
Scorpio   41
Sagittarius   45
Capricorn   49
Aquarius   53
Pisces   57

PLANETARY
REFLECTIONS   61

Mercury   63
Venus   67
Earth   71
Mars   75
Jupiter   79
Saturn   83
Uranus   87
Neptune   91
Pluto   95

ECHOES FROM OUR
CONSTELLATIONS   99

Andromeda   101
Cassiopeia   105
Cygnus   109
Draco   113
Hercules   117
Lyra   121
Orion   125
Pegasus   129
Perseus   133

Dedicated to the feelers.

To the ones who live in the quiet spaces,
feeling more than they ever speak.

This is for you, the ones who wear their
hearts on their sleeves, who feel every
unspoken word, every shift in energy,
every crack in the universe. For the ones
who are moved by the things most people
overlook, who see beauty in the smallest
details, and who carry both the light and
the weight of the world in their hearts.

This is for the ones who sometimes feel like
their heart is too big for their body, who cry
when they're happy, who ache when they
see someone else hurting, who feel the pulse
of the world in every quiet moment. You're
not "too much." You're exactly enough.

*This is for you, the ones who feel it all...because you
know there's something more for you out there.*

Introduction

There comes a time in life when we begin to realize that nothing is ever random. The people we meet, the places we go, the feelings that rise in our hearts—all of it seems to carry meaning, like invisible threads weaving together the story of who we are meant to become. Somewhere along this journey, we are drawn to look up at the sky, searching for something we can't quite put into words. Perhaps it's comfort. Perhaps it's clarity. It might even be a sense that there is something much larger at work, something beyond the everyday moments of life.

You've felt that pull toward something greater, that longing to make sense of the world around you and your role within it. *You are here, reading these words, because you are ready to explore the messages meant just for you.* This is not a coincidence. This is destiny gently nudging you to open your heart to the signs and symbols that have been aligning around you all along.

This is your personal invitation, to pause, to listen, and to connect with the messages the universe has been sending you all along. Why? Well...the planets, the constellations—they've never been just distant lights in the sky. They are reflections of your own journey, echoes of the energy and potential that exist within you. The universe has always been speaking to you, quietly and constantly, guiding you toward a deeper understanding of your place in it all.

When you feel lost, when life feels overwhelming, or when you're simply searching for meaning beyond the day-to-day, let this be a loyal companion. It doesn't offer quick answers or simple fixes. Life hasn't ever been easy. Yet, it offers something much more meaningful... the chance to align with the pulse of the universe and, in turn, *with yourself.* There is something powerful about realizing that the stars you've always admired from afar are not separate from you—they are part of you.

There are messages for you here—messages that were written in the stars long before you even knew to look for them. These messages are about your journey, your heart, your soul's purpose. They are the nudges from the universe reminding you that you are exactly where you need to be, that everything you've experienced has led you to this moment. There is no rush, no race. You are already aligned with the energy, and every step you take is part of a divine plan, whether you can see it clearly or not.

So as you read these pages, take your time. Let the words sink in. Feel the connection between the sky above and the soul within. And most of all, trust that the universe is speaking to you in ways both subtle and profound, guiding you toward the life you are meant to live.

This is the right time to connect with something bigger, to remember that you are part of a beautiful, endless story that stretches across the night sky. You belong here. You always have. The universe has been waiting for you, and now, together, we begin. As you read these pages, take your time. Let the words sink in. Feel the connection between the sky above and the soul within. And most of all, trust that the universe is speaking to you in ways both subtle and profound, guiding you toward the life you are meant to live.

Welcome home.

Zodiac
Whispers

Aries

Adventurous psyche, daring to soar,

Rushing toward the unknown, eager for more,

Intense and fiery, a blaze in the night,

Ever-so enchanted eyes, sparkling with delight,

Silly core, where whimsy freely pours.

AFFIRMATIONS FROM ARIES

My past isn't my definition but my refinement,
forging me into someone stronger and wiser.

The challenges I've faced are the fuel igniting
my courage for whatever comes next.

I seek out souls that stir something deep
within me, where laughter and growth
flow as naturally as breathing.

Scars are stories etched into my skin, testaments
to how fiercely I've lived and loved.

I'm all in—every heartbeat a drumbeat pounding
out the relentless rhythm of "more, more, more."

Aries

LIFE ISN'T MEANT to be lived cautiously, with every step carefully measured and every risk painstakingly avoided. No, life is an adventure to be embraced with wild, unrestrained passion. Embracing life's adventures means accepting the heartbreaks, the failures, and the scars that come from diving in too deep or caring too much. The adventure of life isn't just about the places you go or the things you do; it's about how your essence changes the world around you. It's about seeking souls who challenge you, make you laugh until you cry, and push you to be better and love harder. These people will walk with you through the fire, celebrate when you reach the other side, and remind you that the only way to truly live is to go all in every single time. So, love fiercely. Live wildly. Seek out the experiences that set your soul on fire, chase after them with everything you have, and, as always, enjoy the ride.

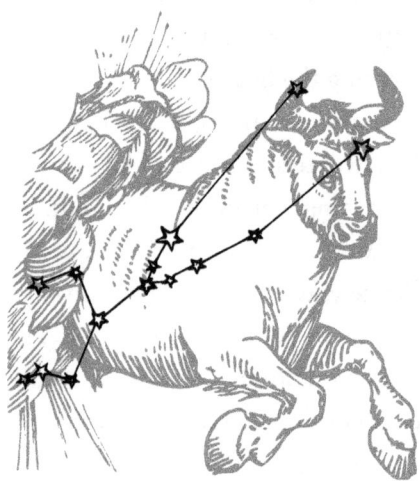

Taurus

Trustworthy, calm, a presence so deep,

Affectionate touches that make hearts leap,

Unwavering support in each step you take,

Reliable always, nothing fake,

Understated grace, elegance so true,

Steady and sure in all that they do.

AFFIRMATIONS FROM TAURUS

I refuse to breathe in toxicity; I will voice my
pain boldly until the world shifts around me.

When everything changes beneath me,
I embrace the breaking ground as the
starting point of endless possibilities.

I am not here to merely 'be okay'; I allow myself to
ignite and rebuild from the ashes on my own terms.

I welcome chaos as my evolution,
transforming the mess of my life into a
masterpiece beyond my imagination.

I don't need to prove my strength by holding
it all together; I permit myself to fall apart and
rise again, more authentic than before.

Taurus

THE OLD MANTRA "keep calm and carry on" seems trite and emotionally cruel today. How can we maintain composure when the ground beneath our feet constantly shifts? This insistence on calm is an unattainable demand to suppress genuine human emotion and mute the distress signals that spur us to action or cry for help. Sometimes, the pressure to stay grounded and cultivate inner peace becomes another burden—a weight that demands we ignore our instincts and mask our true feelings. We're bombarded with quotes urging us to breathe through the pain, but what if the air around us is toxic? This kind of "calm" is not a sanctuary; it's a cell. It isolates us, convincing us that our struggles are ours alone to manage. Resilience requires us to do the opposite of carrying on quietly. Perhaps it's about allowing ourselves to feel full, acknowledge the chaos, and confront the things that disturb our peace so that we can find our own.

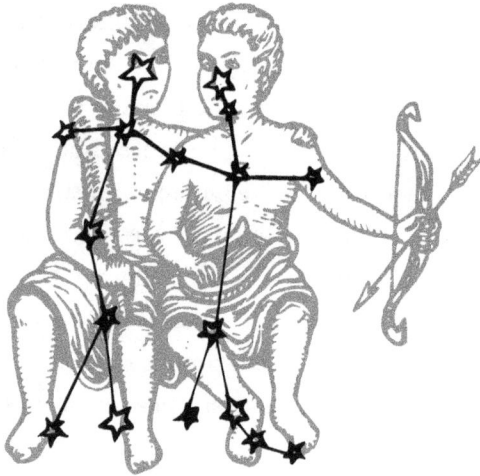

Gemini

Gossip enthusiast, mastering the art,

Energetic, with a brightness that won't depart,

Multitasking master, with flair so vast,

Incredibly engaging, connections that last,

Neighborly vibe, with a warmth that beams,

Intriguingly insightful, with all that gleams.

AFFIRMATIONS
FROM GEMINI

My words have weight, but I am learning to
let them sit before I let them fly. Silence, too,
has power—more than I often realize.

I no longer crave the high of being the one who
knows it all. I find strength in letting things rest where
they belong, without needing to make them mine.

I don't need to stir the pot to be noticed. I
stand out because I know when to sit back.

I will no longer confuse vulnerability with over-
exposure. I reveal myself to those who have
earned the right to see me, and no one else.

I'm done being the one who carries the weight
of what's unsaid. I let go of the need to explain,
justify, or unpack everything for others.

Gemini

I OFTEN FIND MYSELF caught in the act of spilling the tea, only to be hit with a wave of self-doubt immediately after. I truly think my mouth moves faster than my conscience. A part of me thrives on the excitement of knowing things—details about others' lives that feel like little secrets tying us all together. Then there's the nagging voice asking, "Is this really my story to tell?" I don't want to cause harm; it's more about the thrill of connection, of being the one who brings a bit of spice into a conversation. Yet I know there's a fine line between sharing and scathing, and I'm often teetering on the edge. I'm playing with fire, enjoying the moment's warmth while dreading the potential burn.

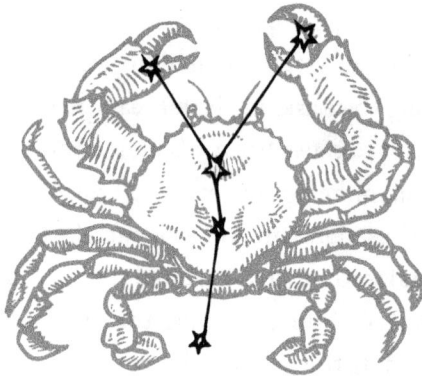

Cancer

Caring and warm, a gentle embrace,

Amicable, soft, a heart of pure grace,

Nurturing friend, in each moment you're there,

Comforting cheer, a solace so rare,

Emotional bonds, deep and sincere,

Remarkable kindness, holding their beloved near.

AFFIRMATIONS
FOR CANCER

I don't seek to be seen by everyone. I crave
to be seen by the few who understand the
parts of me I'm still learning to accept.

I am allowed to protect my dreams. Even if
no one else sees them clearly, I hold them
close because they are mine to nurture.

I see my own fears and I am not ashamed of
them. They are part of what makes me human
and part of what drives me forward.

I give myself permission to rest. I am not
defined by how much I accomplish but by
how well I care for my mind and heart.

I am a work in progress, and that's beautiful.
I am allowed to be both a masterpiece and
a person who is still learning to grow.

Cancer

IN A CROWD, ANYONE CAN look at you. Eyes meet, gazes linger, but to really see someone? Do you notice how their eyes light up when they talk about their favorite person or their love for slow days? That is rare.

It's about understanding the stories hidden behind fake smiles and sad eyes. It's about noticing how someone's laughter changes when they talk about their soulmate or look away just before mentioning their dreams. With these friendships, you don't just meet eyes—you connect worlds. It's the art of seeing not what someone is presenting but what they're protecting. Where others simply look, you see. You see the quirks nobody wants to see, the aspirations whispered to the wind, and the fears they silently swallow. These are the friendships where silence speaks volumes, where a glance can communicate paragraphs. Rare friendships are about being understood without explaining why you see the world the way you do.

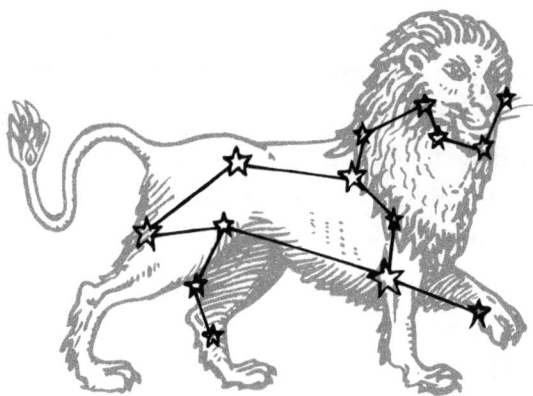

Leo

Loyal and faithful, a beautiful guide,

Energetic and so kind, will never be denied,

Optimistic and bright, forever by your side.

AFFIRMATIONS FOR LEO

My insecurities don't make me less. They make
me more aware, more alive, and ready to burn
through the lies that tell me otherwise.

I am a force of nature. My presence commands attention, not because I demand it, but because I embody
strength, grace, and passion in everything I do.

I will not apologize for the space I take up, nor
shrink myself to make others comfortable. My value
doesn't depend on being palatable or easy to digest.

I've spent too long trying to measure up to
standards that were never meant for me. I don't
need permission to exist in my own greatness, even if it looks nothing like theirs.

I see the cracks in myself that I used to hide. Now,
I stand in the light they let through, unafraid
of being seen—because I finally see myself.

Leo

I SPENT YEARS SILENTLY seething with envy, a dark companion that turned every joyous Instagram post into a personal attack. Each update from a friend—a new job, a beautiful vacation, another engagement—was a direct hit to my self-worth. I'd smile and comment congratulations, but I felt a growing storm of inadequacy and resentment inside. The more I compared, the less I thought I measured up. My achievements seemed trivial and faded when stacked against the brilliant displays on my feed. One night, all at once I realized: my envy wasn't about their happiness but my disbelief in my value and capabilities. I took a hard look at myself, stripped away the comparisons and the self-sabotaging narratives of inadequacy, and began to explore what made me me.

This could have been smoother. There were days I felt exposed, as if peeling back my layers left me vulnerable to even more significant doubts. Gradually, I began to appreciate these parts of myself. First, I tolerated them, then I grew to embrace them, and finally, I celebrated them. I now approach my life with a renewed sense of optimism, not because I'm blind to my flaws but because I'm deeply aware of my worth. Envy occasionally whispers in my ear, but its grip is weak. I am equipped with my own set of extraordinary gifts and committed to living a life that honors them.

Virgo

Visionary thoughts, their head stays clear,

Intellect sharp, wisdom held dear,

Redundant but thoughtful, in each way,

Graceful in manner, through every day,

Original in the life that they steer.

AFFIRMATIONS
FROM VIRGO

I am both creation and destruction. I don't have to
choose one over the other. The beauty of who I am
lies in the way I rise from the path I leave behind.

I don't need the world to understand my balance between structure and spontaneity. I find
my strength in the tension between what I can
control and what I choose to let unfold.

I don't pray for peace—I pray for the strength to hold
my own against the darkness that defines me. The
fight isn't something to win, it's something to live in.

In the moments when I feel overwhelmed, I
trust that my inner calm is still there, waiting for me to find it again when I am ready.

My genius comes from the spaces where
I don't fully understand myself.

Virgo

SOMEWHERE WITHIN ME, there lies a supreme self, eternally at peace, untouched by the chaos that often defines my days. There is a noticeable struggle between my desire for order and the relentless chaos that consumes me. I pray for a version of myself who is eternally at peace, yet reality tells a far more truthful story. There's a violent beauty in the madness that defines me. It's a source of energy, a force that propels me forward even as it threatens to consume me. I'm torn between harnessing this energy and being overwhelmed by it. The walls between inspiration and madness cave in, leaving me questioning my own sanity as I grapple within.

Libra

Loudly loving while living, a joy to behold,

Inspiring all, with stories untold,

Beautiful presence, a radiant glow,

Remarkable warmth, wherever they go,

Amazing and gracious, their life their own.

AFFIRMATIONS
FROM LIBRA

My light comes not from avoiding the shadows,
but from knowing how to rise out of them.

There is no rush to 'be better.' I allow myself the space
to rest, recover, and grow in my own time, knowing that
true healing comes with patience and self-compassion.

The parts of me that still ache are not weak;
they are tender reminders that I have survived,
and survival is nothing less than victory.

I no longer measure my healing by the
absence of pain. I measure it by the way I carry
myself, even with the pain still present.

I put trust in my body and my heart to guide
me. They know what I need to let go of and
what I need to hold onto to keep growing.

Libra

THE MOST BEAUTIFUL people we come across are those who have descended into the depths of defeat, suffering, struggle, and loss, only to emerge with a smile that illuminates everything they encounter. You can sense their aura before you even understand it. It's in how they carry themselves, with quiet confidence and grace. Your very person is discovered at a time when their light is most needed. In a world obsessed with the superficial, let them be your reminder that true beauty lies in the heart and soul, in the scars that tell a story of healing and growth.

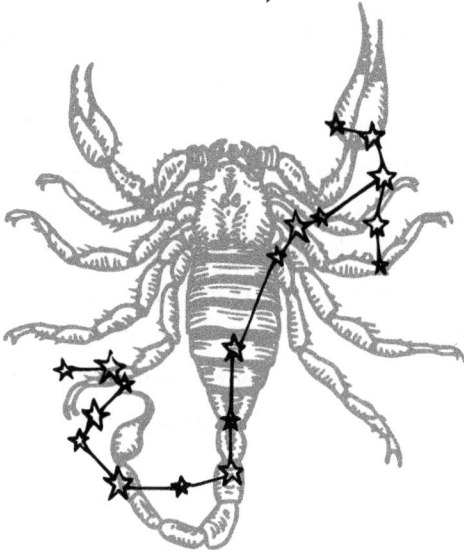

Scorpio

Strong-willed and fierce, a powerful force,

Commanding yet meek, charting life's unsteady course,

Optimistic guide, despite their storms,

Resilient fire, keeping them warm,

Passionate giver, intense and bright,

Intuitive mind, perceiving what's right,

Outstanding presence, a remarkable sight.

AFFIRMATIONS
FROM SCORPIO

Every time I question myself, I'm actually learning
to listen to the parts of me that need the most love.

The mirror may not always reflect someone I
love, but I am learning that self-compassion is
not about instant acceptance. It's about giving
myself permission to be a work in progress.

Some days, I feel completely lost, but that doesn't
mean I'm failing. I can be unsure of my path and
still keep moving forward, step by shaky step.

The chaos and questions that taunt me are not
signs of defeat. They are proof that I am alive,
that I'm still searching, and that there is a part of
me that refuses to settle for less than the truth.

I'm allowed to be angry at the unfairness of it all.
That anger doesn't diminish my ability to heal.

Scorpio

SOME DAYS, THE STRUGGLE to open up is a curse. My heart has been built up and hunkered down from years of self-doubt and self-loathing. It stands guard against a world that seems too harsh and unforgiving. It's easier to stay closed off. The mirror shows a face I sometimes despise, haunted by the fear that my vulnerability weakens me. Life's unfairness slices right through me, a personal attack, each unanswered question a reminder of the pain endured. The enigmas of existence taunt me, chanting that I will never find peace, that the pain is endless, and that I am hopelessly lost within it. Yet, I keep moving forward, driven by a faint, stubborn hope that maybe there's something more waiting for me beyond the shadows.

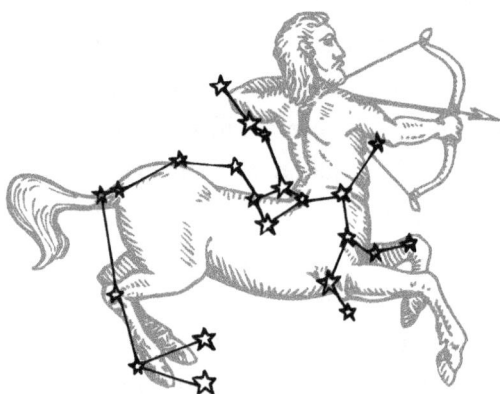

Sagittarius

Seeker of new thrills, adventure in mind,

Aspiring heights, restless and signed,

Generous actions, inspired and kind,

Idealistic flight, unbound and aligned,

Traveling far, thoughts unconfined,

Thirst for new wonders, paths to unwind,

Achieving new highs, their life plan reminds,

Reaching for stars, dreaming so blind,

Imaginative journey, where hope is designed,

Urging forward, leaving limits behind,

Spontaneous being, completely unrefined.

AFFIRMATIONS
FROM SAGITTARIUS

I confront the emptiness I've been running
from. Achievements mean nothing if they
aren't aligned with my soul's desires.

The path I've been following was never mine to
begin with. I am allowed to step off this road, even
if it feels terrifying. I trust my own direction.

I choose to confront my fears, to lean into the
discomfort of choosing myself over everything I
was told I should be. My fulfillment comes from
living boldly, not quietly pleasing others.

I am done with living small. I no longer fear the
unknown path ahead, because it's mine, and I trust
that choosing myself is the bravest thing I can do.

I will not apologize for wanting more
than what's been handed to me.

Sagittarius

CAN YOU EVER REALLY be prepared for the bittersweet truth of reality? Yes, it's true that no matter how much we accomplish, an emptiness can still be lingering. Why? Well...the path we've been following was never designed for our genuine happiness. Seeking approval is fleeting and unpredictable. When we spend our lives chasing it, we lose sight of our own dreams and desires. It's a beautiful illusion, a shiny surface that hides the deeper cracks of unfulfilled potential and forgotten passions. It's time to loudly confront this truth: we've been living for others, not ourselves. Breaking free from the expectations of others and daring to follow our own path is the way to find true fulfillment. Otherwise, we risk a life of empty achievements and quiet dissatisfaction. Choose the path that makes you squirm. Choose yourself.

Capricorn

Committed being, mighty and strong,

Ambitious and hopeful, driven rightfully along,

Practical planner, with a vision so clear,

Righteous in action, showing no fear,

Inspiring others, reaching the sky,

Consistent in efforts, never shy,

Orderly progress, step by step they go,

Responsible leader, bringing grace in tow,

Nobly guiding, their following grows.

AFFIRMATIONS
FROM CAPRICORN

I don't need to feel inspired to stay consistent. I move forward because I know my
strength isn't in the ease of the journey but in
my ability to endure when it gets hard.

Every time I show up for myself, even
when I want to quit, I'm building the kind
of resilience that can't be taught.

I have stopped waiting for the perfect moment to
feel ready. I move forward, flawed and tired, but I
move because I refuse to stay stuck in fear or doubt.

I show up, not because I have to, but because
I know no one else will do this for me.

I don't ask for the road to be easy anymore. I ask
for the strength to keep walking it, knowing that
consistency is what will get me where I need to go.

Capricorn

CONSISTENCY ISN'T PRETTY. It's waking up every morning and knowing that you must do it all over again, with no guarantee that today will be any better than yesterday. It's the nagging doubt that you're wasting your time, that all this effort is for nothing. It's also the stubborn refusal to quit, the determination to see it through, no matter what. Consistency is admitting the truth: the pseudo-motivation you see day in and day out is a filter on reality. It's fleeting and unreliable. It's there when things are going well and disappear when things get complicated. I've had to face some harsh truths on this journey. Admitting that no one is coming to save me, that no one else can do this for me. It's all on me. Does that sound terrifying? It should be frightening. Do you know why? It's empowering in a semi-sadistic way. If I can keep going through the most challenging days...and stay consistent when everything else is falling apart, then there's nothing I can't handle.

Aquarius

Angelic presence, a warm breeze,

Quintessential charm, putting minds at ease,

Unique in spirit, one-of-a-kind,

Accelerated thinker, exploring the mind,

Revolutionary thoughts, ahead of their time,

Insights on truth, the deepest to find,

Uplifting others, with their grace,

Sporadic actions, setting their pace.

AFFIRMATION
FOR AQUARIUS

I don't apologize for taking the quieter path. I know
the value of choosing my peace, my joy, and my growth,
even when it doesn't align with what the world expects.

My life, my decisions, and my
peace are mine to protect.

The things that ground me—my habits,
my moments of calm—are not small.

I no longer seek the spotlight, because
I am my own source of light.

I trust the power in my subtle choices, in the
way I show up for myself daily, knowing that
true strength is not measured by how loud I can
be but by how deeply I believe in myself.

Aquarius

HAVE YOU EVER encountered someone whose very presence seems to carry a quiet defiance against the norms? They might not stand out in the most visible ways, but there's something about them—a certain ease in their skin and a subtle yet unshakable confidence that draws you. The subtle you-got-this nods, the fleeting moments where they choose kindness over criticism. It's in the way they might laugh at themselves when they get something wrong or how they can turn a seemingly insignificant detail—a favorite phrase, a daily ritual—into something that grounds them, that brings comfort in a chaotic world. For them, it's an unspoken understanding that it's okay to not have it all figured out. They might not always take the path most traveled, but they're at peace with that choice. They're the ones who, when faced with a tough day, will opt for a simple pleasure because they know that it's the little things that get us through.

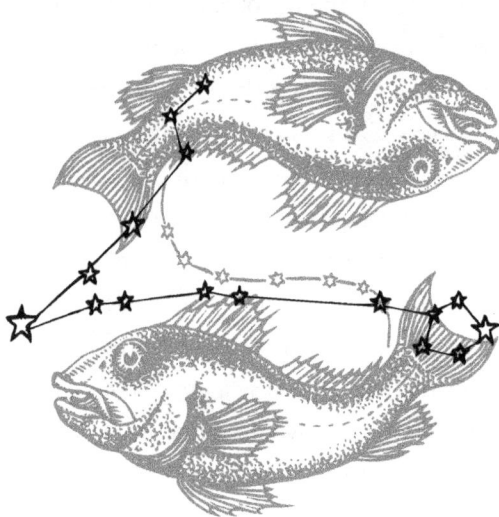

Pisces

Peaceful nature, calm and serene,

Inspirational presence, darks guiding beam,

Sensitive empath, with love to show,

Compassion flows, everywhere they go,

Empathetic yet un-cold, feeling deep below,

Serendipity is found in life's gentle blows.

AFFIRMATIONS FROM PISCES

I am learning that my kindness does not
have to deplete me. I can give to others
while still keeping enough for myself.

I release the need to be everything for everyone. My
value is not measured by how much I give away.

I deserve to care for myself with the same compassion I offer others. My kindness includes
me, and I no longer apologize for that.

Protecting my energy is an act of self-
love, and I owe that to myself.

I will no longer allow kindness to drain me. I choose
to give from a place of abundance, not exhaustion.

Pisces

BEING KIND BEARS US with a burden that sometimes feels almost too much to swallow. Kindness isn't always the pure, saintly act it's made out to be. Keeping the peace is a delicate chain that tightens with every piece of yourself that you give away. People often take and take, mistaking deep kindness for an endless well. They say character is destiny, and if that's true, mine has been to give until I felt like I might fade away, becoming a shadow of who I once was, haunted by the kindness I couldn't stop offering. I'm not powerless against it. I can feel the strain, see the cracks forming, and know that something must change. I've been patient, understanding, and empathetic to a fault, and yes, it has left me so very tired. Emotions, as relentless as they are, also hold the key to a whole life. They don't disappear because we wish them away, but they don't have to consume us. I'm beginning to understand that it's okay to feel, be angry, hurt, and prioritize myself when I need to. I'm learning to care for myself and to put my needs first without the shadow of guilt looming over me. With that realization comes hope. I'm starting to thrive.

Planetary
Reflections

Mercury

Mysterious thoughts unraveled,
with every word spoken,

Enlightening our minds, bridging
spaces once never opened,

Relentlessly from the ashes,
their spirit never broken,

Curator of conversations
that the heart defines,

Unseen demons, yet always kind,

Remarkable their battles,
opportunities to refine,

Yearning for kindness, for
their soul to unwind.

AFFIRMATIONS
FROM MERCURY

I am done being a well others can drink from
endlessly. My kindness will no longer be my
burden. I give only what nourishes me first.

They have no idea what it's taken to be here today. The
shadows I carry are a testament to my resilience, and
every moment I choose myself, I become untouchable.

I no longer wait for permission to prioritize myself. I am my own protector.

I honor the kindness within me, even when life
has tried to steal it. I am learning to balance my
empathy with boundaries that protect my heart.

I am more than my past. The hurt I've experienced
has made me wiser, and I use that wisdom to build
a future that reflects the love and light I deserve.

Mercury

WE ALL KNOW SOMEONE like this, but do we really see them? The kindest souls often carry the heaviest burdens, yet you'd never know by looking at them. They don't share the things that haunt their nights—the memories that play like a silent film in their minds, the tongue they swallow to keep the peace, the hands that should have held but instead hurt. They've been hurt, their innocence burned away by betrayals that cut deeper than any knife. They've been used, left to gather the shattered pieces of a life they never asked for. They've witnessed the darkest sides of humanity—up close, too close—and it's left them with a shadow they can't escape, a darkness that lingers no matter how far they go. It's the kind of acceptance that sees through the lies that don't have time for excuses. They've faced the worst and don't entertain drama, fake smiles, or empty gestures. They're unshaken by anger, tears, or desperation because they've been there. They've cried into the void, felt rock bottom's chilling emptiness, and survived.

Even after all that, they're here to help you survive, too.

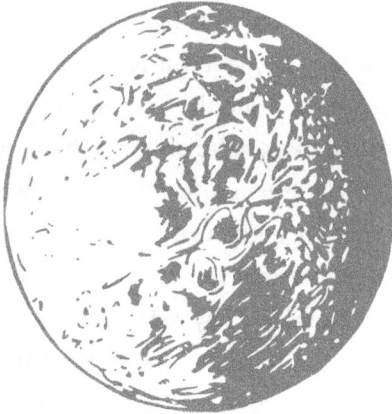

Venus

Visionary of beauty, an allure that invites

Embodying all that is deep, sexy, and kind,

Nurturing all with gentle ease,

Undying attention to those in need,

Sensual beings, wearing their hearts on their sleeves.

AFFIRMATIONS
FROM VENUS

I trust myself to recognize when I need to pull back. I
am not at the mercy of anyone else's games or control.

I am not defined by anyone's attention or
lack of it. My worth is inherent, and I refuse to beg for validation or affection.

I choose who I let into my thoughts, my heart,
and my space. That choice is always mine, no matter how overwhelming the attraction may feel.

I honor my boundaries, knowing that
my self-respect will always come before
any fleeting desire or attraction.

I stand rooted in my own autonomy. My body, my
mind, my choices—they belong to me, and no one else.

Venus

THEIR PRESENCE. Their presence is an assault on every sense, an intrusion you welcome and fear in equal measure. They don't need to speak for you to feel it; it's in the way they carry themselves, a confidence that borders on arrogance, a knowledge that they could have you if they wanted, and you'd let them—no, you'd beg them. Your thoughts are no longer your own. They've taken them over, filling your mind with images, fantasies, and things you shouldn't want but can't help craving.

They know it, too—they see the power they have over you, and it only makes them more dangerous, more desirable. They play with it, with you, a cat toying with a mouse, pushing you to the edge, and pulling back just before you fall. It's torture, exquisite, and unbearable, and you find yourself craving more of it. More of them... even though you know it will destroy you in ways you'll never recover from.

Earth

Encompassing life in abundant display,

Accepting what matters most in times of dismay,

Resilient beings, leading the way,

Thriving amongst the chaos, seizing the day

Harboring beauty through the wind's gentle sway

AFFIRMATIONS
FROM EARTH

I am not just existing in this world—I am shaping it. Every thought I have, every decision I make, creates ripples that extend far beyond what I can see.

The universe flows through me, not around me. My breath, my heartbeat—they are not just signs of life; they are evidence of the energy I harness every day.

I don't search for peace or purpose outside of myself, because I know that everything I need is already within me. I am the calm and the storm.

I am not here by accident, and I do not move through life passively. I bend the world to my will because I know the strength within me.

I am not waiting for my time—it is now. Every action I take is aligned with my purpose, and every moment is an opportunity for me to expand my power.

Earth

THERE IS A STORY IN the soil beneath your feet, in the trees that stand as silent witnesses to the passage of time. When you take the time to listen—to really listen—you find that the world is not just something you move through but something you are a part of. This is where the magic lies. It's in the simple act of being present. It's in the way the earth smells after rain, the sun warms your skin, and the stars remind you of your place in the universe. With this, you find a sense of belonging, peace, and a profound understanding that you are not just in the world—you are the world.

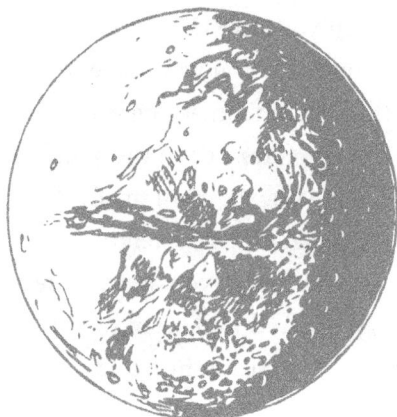

Mars

Mighty and ambitious, fiercely ablaze,

Assertive in nature, often unphased,

Righteous warrior, knowing their worth,

Soulful creatures, with goals that move forth.

AFFIRMATIONS
FROM MARS

Every day is a chance to be more than I was yesterday.

I don't wait for perfect conditions. I create my
own opportunities, even in the middle of chaos,
because I am capable of thriving anywhere.

My standards are my own, and I will not shrink
myself to fit someone else's definition of success.

I'm not interested in halfway. I commit fully,
knowing that even when I stumble, I rise stronger, because I demand the best from myself.

I won't wait for an opportunity to knock—I build
the door. I am the creator of my own success,
and nothing holds me back but myself.

Mars

YOU'RE NOT HERE TO BE cautious, to be timid. You're here to make waves, set fires, and leave something behind that screams you were here, that you mattered. Pour your heart out into whatever you're doing. Feel it in your bones; let it burn through your veins until there's nothing left but the raw, relentless force of your will. You're not made for mediocrity. You're not built to settle for "good enough." You're crafted from the same stuff as the stars, forged in the crucible of existence. Act like it. Demand greatness from yourself, not because you want it easy, but because you want better. You'll know you didn't just exist when you've given everything. You lived.

Jupiter

Jovial and grand, accepting of all,

Unparalleled and bold, to rise and not fall,

Protector of secrets, the one you call,

Intense, and magnetic, tempting
energy you could never withdraw,

Tender-hearted exchanges,
where kindness outlaws all,

Extravagant gestures, with
the joy they sprawl,

Radiating gold, their presence ethereal.

AFFIRMATIONS
FROM JUPITER

I do not seek perfection, in love or in life. I
seek truth, connection, and the courage to
be vulnerable, even when it feels hard.

I seek love that sees me for who I am, that holds
space for me to heal and become more.

I am worthy of love that accepts me fully, and
I no longer need to hide my scars or imperfections. They are part of what makes me whole.

I am the source of love and I attract it by simply being
who I am—whole, powerful, and unapologetically me.

I am not afraid to lose in love because I
know that in the end, I will always have
myself. I am my own foundation.

Jupiter

LOVE. LOVE IS NOT FOR THE faint of heart. It's not the romanticized version we're fed but something more brutal and honest. It's standing in front of someone with all your wounds exposed, knowing they see every scar, every broken piece, and still, they stay. Being in love doesn't come without pain. It's earned in the moments when you want to walk away when the weight of it all feels too heavy, but you choose to stay. It knows that love isn't about finding someone who makes you whole but about finding someone who sees you as you are and holds space for you to heal, grow, and become more than you ever thought you could be. Love is messy and un-comfortable. It's where you find out what you're really made of and what you're really willing to fight. There's a kind of experience that can't be taught, only approached with caution. It's about showing up daily, saying, "This is who I choose. Again, and again, and forever...you."

Saturn

Sensible choices, logic's unmistakable voice,

Admirable actions, drowning out noise,

Tenacity unmatched, firm and poised,

Unwavering faith, never destroyed

Remarkable perception, subtle and coy,

Natural-born leaders, the confidence they enjoy.

AFFIRMATIONS FROM SATURN

I stand at the edge of this choice, knowing it will fracture who I've been, but within that breaking lies the chance to become who I was always meant to be.

I'm stepping into this choice fully aware of the cost, but I trust that what I'm building within myself is far more powerful than what I leave behind.

I remind myself that destruction is a form of creation. What breaks me now is only clearing space for something far more powerful to emerge.

I do not fear pain or uncertainty, I fear stagnation. I will not stand still when I know I am meant to move

I am my greatest asset, my deepest strength, and my fiercest ally. There's no need to seek validation from the outside because everything I need to thrive is already within me. I am my own foundation.

Saturn

LIFE WILL CORNER YOU, and every choice will feel as if it's pulling pieces of your soul apart. It will never be about finding an easy escape—it's about choosing the path that changes you because, deep down, you know it's the only way forward. You're facing a decision that will hurt and might leave you with scars, but you choose it anyway. There's no glory here, only the grit to keep moving because giving up or backing down would cost you far more. You're giving up comfort, security, and maybe even a piece of yourself for something you can't fully grasp yet. It's survival in its rawest form—you against your own fears and doubts. These choices strip away what's unnecessary, leaving you vulnerable and exposed. But in that vulnerability, there's strength. After all, no guts, no glory. And maybe that's the point. Maybe the hardest, most painful choices are the ones that force you to confront yourself and find out who you really are when there's nothing left but the fight.

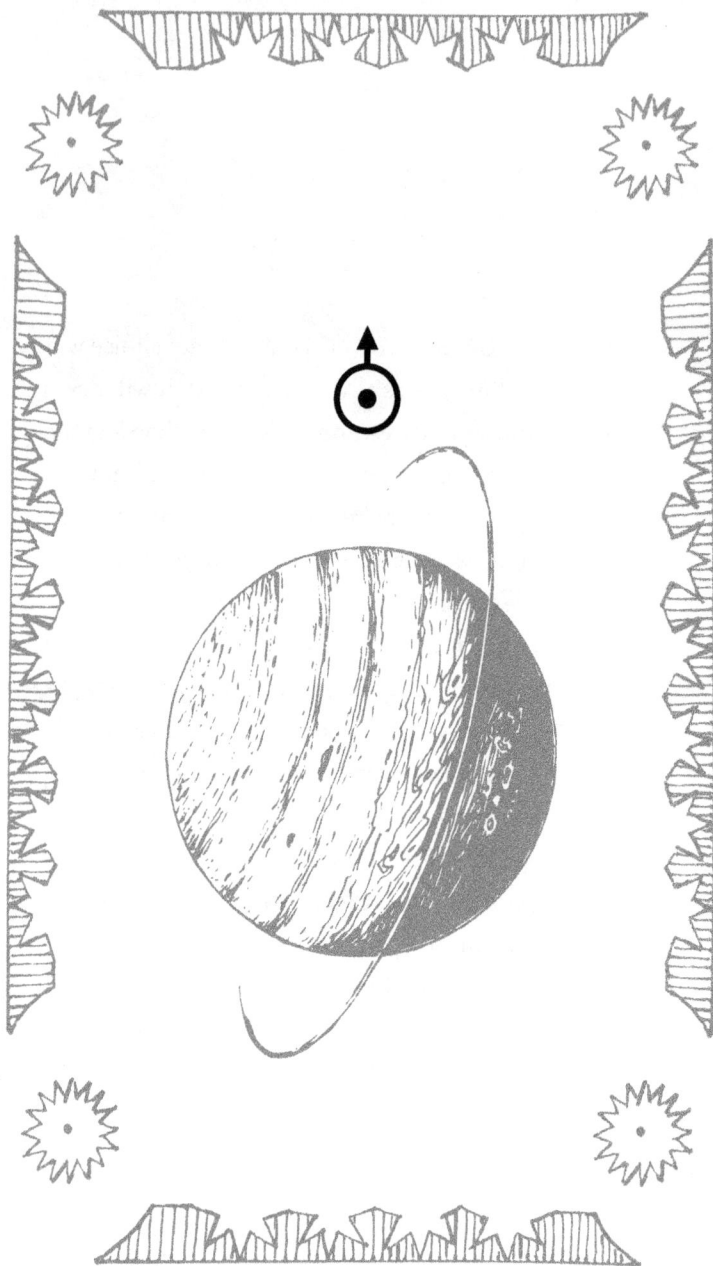

Uranus

Unrelinquished creatives, you name it, there's art,

Rebelling against norms, they know their part,

Adventurous streaks, exploring the departed,

Non-conformist paths, courageously started,

Unique in each way, setting trends, never in tow,

Sparking hope, so boldly they glow.

AFFIRMATIONS
FROM URANUS

My truth is not negotiable, and I will not apologize
for the chaos that comes with being fully alive.

The only validation I need is my own, and it will never
again be up for sale. My worth is not a bargaining
chip, and I refuse to be valued by anyone but myself.

I reclaim the parts of myself that I
abandoned for the sake of fitting in, and
in doing so, I become whole again.

I move with intention and leave behind anything that no longer serves me, with no guilt
for the things that once held meaning.

I will unlearn everything they taught me
about who I'm supposed to be. My truth isn't
bound by lessons handed down—it's birthed
in the wild space where nothing is certain.

Uranus

SIT IN SILENCE, KEEP your head down, and be what everyone else wants you to be. From the start, you're fed this lie: if you just follow the script—if you're quiet, if you don't make waves, if you walk the walk set out for you—you'll find your place. I bought into that lie, convinced myself that if I could just mute the parts of me that were too loud, too opinionated, too different, then I'd finally be accepted.

For what? To be accepted by people who wouldn't even recognize the real me if I slapped them in the face with it? To be part of a crowd that would rather see me as a carbon copy than as the chaotic, messy, too-much-to-handle person I am? I was a shell of myself that looked the part but felt empty inside, constantly craving approval that never mattered. It took me far too long to see I was simply trading pieces of my soul for scraps of validation, and it wasn't enough. It was never going to be enough. I'd instead burn their whole playbook to the ground and be unapologetically, brutally myself than ever go back to being a stranger in my own life.

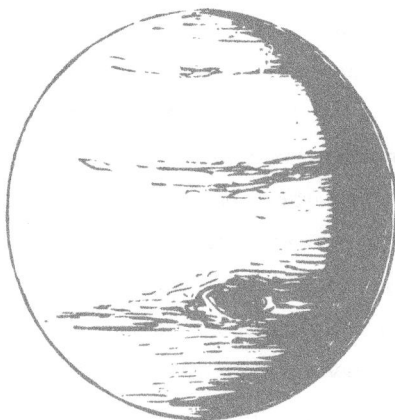

Neptune

Nebular mindset, you know the gist,

Empathy's whisperer, life's subtle mist,

Profound echoes from the above call,

Tranquil moments where secrets are loved,

Unseen realms of ethereal dreams, never ignored,

Nirvanic journeys, through the stars soared,

Ethereal union, bridging the cosmic and all.

AFFIRMATIONS
FROM NEPTUNE

I release the need to impress or achieve for
others. The only applause I seek is my own
deep sigh of peace at the end of each day.

Today I let go of the chase for more,
understanding that my happiness grows in the
space where I allow life to unfold naturally.

I no longer believe in the myth of 'someday.'
Contentment is in the small, quiet
moments I allow myself to embrace.

I will no longer burden myself with expectations. I've
simplified, and in that simplicity, I've found myself.

I am enough at this moment, just as I am.
Happiness isn't something I will need to chase—
it's already here, waiting for me to notice.

Neptune

YOU THOUGHT YOU NEEDED to be more successful, impressive, and everything. Somewhere along the way, you realize that all you want is something much more straightforward and purer. You just want to be happy.

You want the kind of happiness that doesn't come with a round of applause but with a gentle sigh of contentment at the end of the day. It's the kind of happiness that slips through your fingers when you try to grasp it too hard but lingers softly when you let it be. You've stripped it all down to what really matters. You've let go of the bullshit—the expectations, the pressure to be something you're not. You've realized that happiness isn't something you find in the future, in some distant place, once you've accomplished enough or become enough. It's here, right now, in the life you're living.

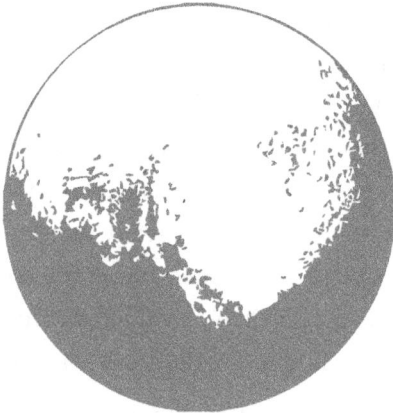

Pluto

Positive force, transforming through strife,

Liberating depths, unveiling through life,

Unseen shadows, with truth to impart,

Transcendent journey, a rebirth of the heart,

Orchestrator of power, tearing the bounds of darkness apart.

AFFIRMATIONS
FROM PLUTO

I'm done looking for someone to save me.
The only person capable of carrying me
through this is the one I see in the mirror.

I don't need an audience for my own liberation. This
is my quiet revolution. No crowds, no spectacle.
Just me, choosing to exist on my own terms.

I stopped looking for a way out when I realized
the only way through is with myself. I don't
need to escape—I need to trust that even
in my most fractured state, I'm whole.

I am not waiting for the stars to align. I create my own
constellations, and my sky belongs to no one else.

I tell myself that every error was part of the process,
not the definition of who I am becoming.

Pluto

ONE MOMENT, EVERYTHING seems clear, and the next, you're on your knees, feeling the weight of change, surrounded by the pieces of who you used to be. Don't let this be a moment to only let go. This is what choosing yourself is, an emotional, messy, profound experience that invites you to release what no longer serves you. It's not easy but it's necessary—it's a slow, careful unfolding that asks you to meet the parts of yourself you've been avoiding with the dignity and grace you deserve.

When you finally emerge, you're not who you were before. You're changed, carrying the quiet strength of someone who has faced their shadows and found light on the other side. This is what rebirth truly is—not a dramatic transformation but a soft, steady emergence into a new way of being. It's the soft realization that, despite everything, you're still here, breathing and becoming. And in that, there is a quiet, profound beauty.

Echoes
From Our
Constellations

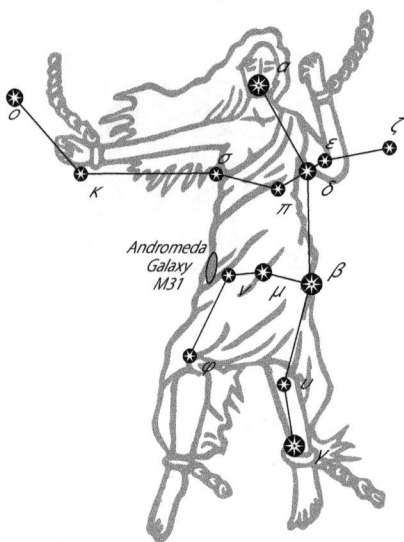

Andromeda
Galaxy
M31

Andromeda

Assistant of higher realms, their vision crystal clear,

Nonconforming and demure, spreading love without fear.

Driven by compassion, with empathy vast,

Receptive and wise, drawing from their past.

Optimistic beings, bringing light to the unknown,

Mysterious and intuitive, in wisdom, they're grown.

Elevated in thought, with insight so rare,

Demulcent and beautiful, they genuinely care.

Authentic and true, inspiring everywhere.

AFFIRMATIONS
FROM ANDROMEDA

I honor my emotions, knowing they are
valid and deserve to be felt, not hidden.

I won't force myself into the light when I
need to rest in the shadows. My emotions
deserve space, not suppression.

I release the expectation that I have to be
'okay' right now. I am worthy, even in my
struggles, even when I feel stuck.

Today, I'm choosing to just be, without forcing progress.

If I don't have it in me, that's where I'm
staying, and for that, I am at peace.

Andromeda

SOME DAYS, YOU WAKE UP and everything feels off. There's this heavy weight pressing down on your chest. You call it a funk, fear, or whatever name makes it feel less monstrous. But the truth is, it's overwhelming and colors everything in shades of gray. The first instinct? Fake it. Plaster on a smile, force yourself through the motions, and tell everyone—and yourself—that you're okay. We've been taught to do this, smooth over the rough edges and present a face to the world that says, "I'm okay," even when you're anything but.

Faking it? It's a trap. It's toxic positivity at its most insidious, convincing you that your pain isn't valid, that you don't have the right to feel what you're feeling. It's about shoving your real emotions into a box, locking them away, and hoping that if you ignore them long enough, they'll disappear. What if, instead, you gave yourself permission to feel? To let the fear, the sadness, the anxiety, just be? What if you took a step back, took it easy, and stopped forcing yourself to pretend everything's okay when it's not? Better days are coming, sure, but that doesn't mean today has to be one of them. You don't have to force yourself into the light when unready. You don't have to fake a smile. It tries to paint over your pain with bright colors, yet healing happens when you sit with the darkness and let yourself be exactly where you are without trying to rush to where you think you should be.

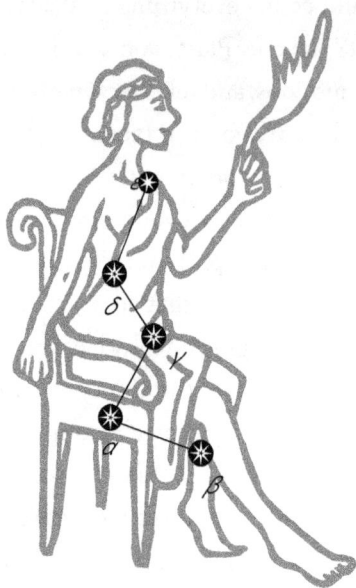

Cassiopeia

Captivating presence, a beauty so profound,

Adoring eyes, where gentleness is found

Serenity in their gaze, a peaceful allure,

Supreme elegance, their charm so pure.

Intrinsic grace, in every move they make,

Opulent charm, impossible to fake.

Profound insight, deep truths they partake,

Elegant demeanor, in every step they take,

Illusive, a whisper in the breeze,

Aspiring mind, forever seeks to seize.

AFFIRMATIONS
FROM CASSIOPEIA

There is power in surrender, a beauty in giving
myself to moments that move me, trusting that
each experience shapes me with purpose.

In you, I see both the calm and the tempest,
and I accept both, knowing that love in its
truest form is never one without the other.

Our connection is a secret the world cannot
understand, and in that mystery, I find the
strength to love with all my heart.

In the presence of your soul, I feel both
vulnerable and powerful, knowing that love
this deep can only make me stronger.

Your soul speaks to mine in a language beyond
words, and I find trust in the way it draws me
closer, even when the path is uncertain.

Cassiopeia

THE WAY YOU SMILE reminds me of a secret only we share, a trick that pulls me closer with every glance. Your soul wraps around me, kissing me with a gentle whisper, promising comfort and connection in a way that words could never capture. There's a fire in you, a quiet yet intense passion that ignites something deep inside me, something that craves to be near your presence, to bask in the energy only you can give. Every moment with you is beautiful surrender, a pull that I can't and don't want to resist.

Yet, beneath the surface of that comfort lies a truth we both choose to ignore: you're the storm that will one day tear me apart, and I'll welcome the devastation with open arms, because even in destruction, I'd rather feel you than feel nothing at all.

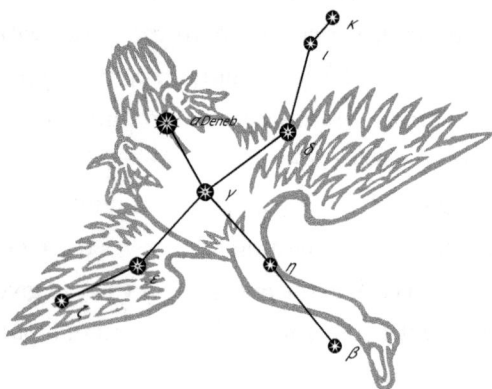

Cygnus

Contagious in essence, beauty not just skin-deep,

Yearning always for the depths, where dark secrets sleep,

Genuine and true, to all they greet,

Notoriously tender, their words match their face,

Undeterred in their strength, it graces the world with heavenly trace,

Sensational presence, soaring with timeless grace.

AFFIRMATIONS
FROM CYGNUS

I embrace the irony of growth—that in
trying to escape the unknown, I found that
I had everything I needed all along.

The more I venture out, the more I see how
little I truly understand—and there's deep
beauty in accepting that ignorance.

The boundaries I once felt confined by were never
physical—they were the limits I placed on myself.
Now, I welcome the limitlessness of who I am.

I find myself expanding in ways that
routine could never offer me.

I understand now that the wisdom I was searching
for isn't found in revelation, but in my willingness
to continuously question and explore.

Cygnus

THERE WAS A TIME WHEN I clung to the comforting cogs of routine, bound by the familiar and safe. Yet, a persistent whisper from within urged me to seek beyond these boundaries, to discover what lies beyond my comfort zone. I began to make space in my life for the new and untested. With each small venture, I found not just new sights and sounds but new depths to my own soul. The world expanded before me with possibilities that once seemed beyond reach in the palm of my hand. Now, I cherish every new encounter, every unexpected challenge, and every lesson learned in the boldness of exploration. This journey has taught me that true growth is not about discarding what I once knew, but rather, making it more beautiful. It's funny how I thought venturing beyond my comfort zone would lead to some grand revelation, some life-altering wisdom. Instead, I've found myself caught in a cycle of strange ironies—every step forward reveals just how little I actually know. The more I explore, the more I realize that the boundaries I was so desperate to break were never really holding me back. It turns out, the biggest challenge wasn't the unknown, but accepting that all the answers I was searching for were right there in the mess I was trying to escape.

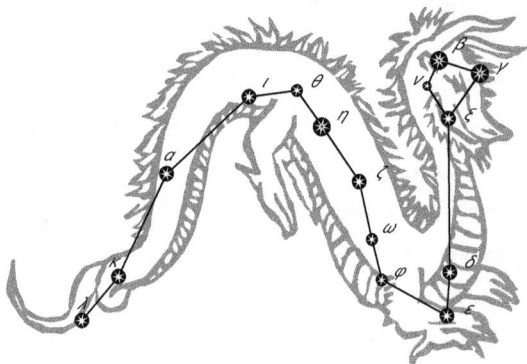

Draco

Delicate in thought, with a mind so keen,

Reflective and deep, in shadows unseen.

Artistic and sensual, emotions entwine,

Chaotic presence, a force so divine.

Ominous allure, with secrets that define.

AFFIRMATIONS
FROM DRACO

I navigate life like a lucid dreamer, choosing when
to dive deep and when to drift along the surface.

I exist in the balance between connection and solitude,
untouched by the chaos yet fully aware of it.

I am the quiet observer of my own life, grounded
in a stillness that no external noise can shatter.

I flow with the currents of the world, but my anchor is
always within reach, ready to steady me when needed.

I protect the untouched spaces of my soul, where the
world's reach ends and my essence remains untouched.

Draco

LIFE IS SUCH A STRANGE thing to grasp. I see it clearly, a dream just beyond a glass wall—close enough to touch, yet distant enough that I don't lose myself in it. It's a constant negotiation between engagement and detachment. I am here, in the thick of it, feeling every pulse of the world around me, yet I keep a part of myself separate, untouched, and unscathed. I'm neither fully immersed nor entirely withdrawn; I hover in that space where I can observe without being overwhelmed. Some days, the pull is stronger, the world louder, demanding more of me than I want to give. On those days, I draw back, retreating into the quiet corners of my mind, where I can regroup and remind myself of who I am—of the core that stays intact no matter how much I give away. I let the world swirl around me, knowing I can step back whenever I choose, but only when I am ready.

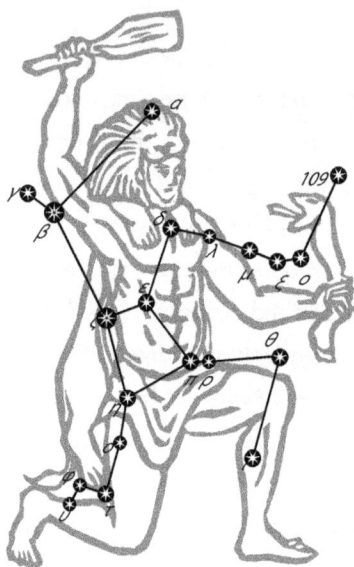

Hercules

Heroic in jest, inspiring all they meet,

Empowering, lifting others to their feet.

Rigid in principles, unwavering and true,

Consistent in actions, through and through.

Undeterred by setbacks, their resolve is firm as stone,

Lawful, honoring codes they've always known.

Earnest in every endeavor, their sincerity clear,

Steadfast with commitment, devoid of all fear.

AFFIRMATIONS
FOR HERCULES

I don't need to save the world; my power comes from
saving space for my own growth and well-being.

I challenge the narrative that strength means carrying
it all—real power is knowing when to let go.

By letting go of who I 'should' be, I discover
the quiet power of simply being myself.

I choose to step out of the legend others wrote
for me and live the story that unfolds within.

I find my power not in being invincible, but in
embracing the uncertainty of every moment with grace.

Hercules

Wouldn't we all want to be the hero? I mean, isn't that what we were told growing up? We should aim to be the best, the one who always steps up, never falters, and everyone can count on. This idea got planted in us early on that we're supposed to be these larger-than-life figures, carrying the world's weight on our shoulders. Wouldn't we all love to be the one who saves the day? Sure. But that's not the reality, and it's not what we should be holding ourselves—or anyone else—to. We're told we should be these perfect versions of ourselves, but who does that serve? Not us. We're all just people trying to do our best, and that's more than enough to be the hero of your own story.

We were never meant to carry the weight of the world. This notion that we have to be everything, do everything, and save everyone is a false story we've been told. The truth is, we aren't here to be perfect, or invincible, or always in control. We're here to be real, to feel deeply, to learn as we go.

Heroism is in the vulnerability of simply being who you are, not who the world has told you to be.

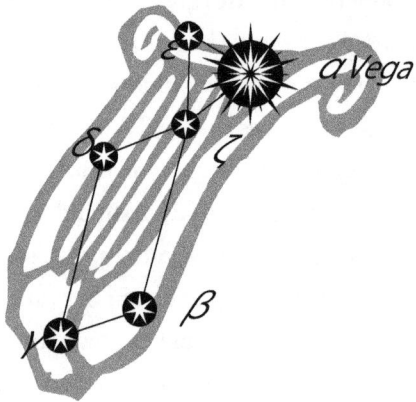

Lyra

Lavish in verse, her words dance with ease,

Youthful spark, forever aiming to please.

Reassuring presence, a calm in every storm,

Appreciative like no other, a soul so warm.

AFFIRMATIONS
FROM LYRA

No matter how dim it may seem, my inner light never
fades—it is always there, waiting for me to reignite it.

I don't need to be saved; I hold the power within me
to rise and nurture the spark that's always been mine.

I embrace the truth that my light has no obligation
to be seen by others—it shines for me first.

I trust in my ability to illuminate even the darkest parts
of myself, knowing that darkness and light can coexist.

Even in moments of uncertainty, I know
that I am capable of finding my way.

Lyra

There's a light in you, even if you can't see it right now.

Then they left.

The words hit me. Cutting through the heavy darkness that had become my second skin. It was like they reached inside me, grasping at that last, fragile spark I'd buried so deep I almost forgot it was there. For a moment, everything stopped—the weight, the noise. That spark flickered, uncertain, but it was there, refusing to die out. As much as I wanted to deny it, I couldn't shake the feeling that maybe, just maybe, there was someone worth fighting for after all.

For the first time in what felt like forever, I didn't feel completely lost. Maybe, just maybe, they were right. Maybe there was something left in me, something worth nurturing, something worth saving. And that light—no matter how small, no matter how buried—was still mine. It had never left. It was waiting, patiently, for me to believe in it again.

At that moment, I realized: it wasn't about being saved by someone else. It was about realizing I could save myself.

Betelgeuse

βRigel

Orion

Optimistic in pursuit, a leader in every trial,

Resilient in adversity, never too frail.

Impassioned with vigor, a heart of steel,

Outspoken and daring, their spirit prevails.

Noble in purpose, their actions entail.

AFFIRMATIONS
FROM ORION

I recognize that my voice is a powerful instrument
of change, and I choose to use it fearlessly
to challenge norms and inspire others.

Embracing the discomfort that comes with
speaking my truth, I understand that growth and
progress are born from courageous honesty.

I honor the unique perspectives that I bring to the
world, knowing that my authentic expression adds
value and ignites meaningful conversations.

I refuse to let fear or societal expectations silence
me; my words are a reflection of my true self and
have the power to create ripples of positive change.

By standing firm in my convictions and sharing my
ideas openly, I empower not only myself but also
those around me to live boldly and authentically.

Orion

Outspoken souls understand the power of words. They know that speaking up isn't always about being the loudest in the room but rather about being the realest. It's about having the courage to express ideas that might be unpopular or uncomfortable but are essential for progress. These souls are not afraid of the discomfort that sometimes comes with being direct because they know this discomfort is the birthplace of change. They remind us all that actual progress is born from the voices that dare to be heard, from the hearts that refuse to be silenced. Keep shining, keep speaking, and know that your voice is a powerful force for change. If they can do it, you should, too.

Silence will never protect you. Silence will never carry your truth into the light. But your voice—your voice is power. It's rebellion and revelation, all at once. The world will try to tell you to be quiet, to fit in, to smooth your edges. Don't listen. The world has enough echoes. What it needs is the rawness of your truth, the fierceness of your heart, and the audacity of your voice.

So speak, not because you have permission, but because you have purpose. Speak because your words are the fire that someone else needs to find their own. And when you do, when you rise with that unshakable resolve, you'll realize that the most powerful thing you could ever do is simply to refuse to be silent.

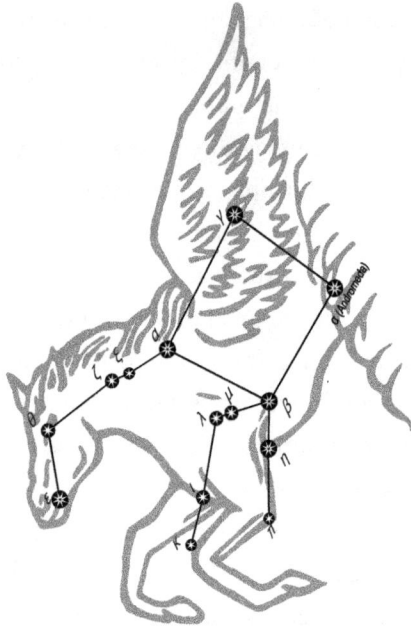

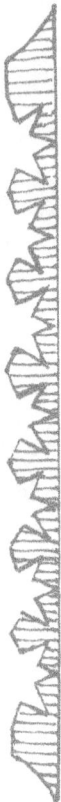

Pegasus

Poetic in essence, their tales on overdrive,

Electric charm, lighting up the sky.

Gracious and graceful, with every beat of their wings,

Affirming hope, their words won't sting,

Stirring in stories, with that tales delight the senses,

Unfaltering might, their soul never waivers.

Sensational allure, in all the right places.

AFFIRMATIONS
FROM PEGASUS

I embrace the profound awakenings sparked
by transformative connections, allowing them
to reveal the deepest parts of my soul.

Even when paths diverge, I honor the indelible
impact of meaningful encounters, using their
legacy to fuel my personal evolution.

The intensity of my emotions is a testament to
my capacity for deep love and passion, which I
carry forward with strength and gratitude.

I choose to see departures not as losses but as
gifts that have enriched my journey, reminding
me of the boundless potential within me.

Forever changed and empowered, I carry the
essence of impactful experiences within me,
using them to illuminate my path ahead.

Pegasus

EXPERIENCING YOUR TWIN soul isn't for the weak. They come into your life suddenly, and nothing is the same from that moment. There's a connection so deep, so intense, it shakes you to your core. They inspire, challenge, and make you feel things you didn't even know you could feel. For a short while, everything is precisely as it should be.

Well, they leave, and it feels like your world is ripped apart. The emptiness they leave behind is absolute but not a loss. It's a wake-up call, a reminder of what you're capable of, of the kind of love and passion you can experience. They weren't meant to stay—they were meant to show you what you've been missing, to build something within you that you can carry forward. When you stand in the aftermath, broken but awakened, please realize their presence was a gift. They showed you the depths of your soul, and in their absence, you find the strength to continue. You carry their memory not as a wound but as a reminder of the love that once filled you, knowing that it's now a part of who you are—forever changed, forever stronger.

Perseus

Protective in nature, shielding the weak,

Empathetic eyes, secrets they keep.

Relentless darkness, battles unseen,

Sorrow's companion, where hope has been.

Eloquent silence, bearing old scars,

Unyielding prayers, beneath the stars.

Sincere guardian, with tears unshed.

AFFIRMATIONS FROM PERSEUS

I choose to live fully by allowing my heart
to feel deeply, embracing vulnerability
as a courageous act of self-love.

My past pain has shaped me but does not confine
me; I open myself to connections that celebrate
my authentic self, imperfections and all.

I dismantle the walls around my heart,
trusting that true strength lies in welcoming
love, even when it feels risky.

Each day, I honor my resilience by letting
others see me wholly, knowing that I deserve
to be seen, heard, and cherished.

I transform fear into grace, allowing my heart
to be a vessel for love, compassion, and the
profound connections that enrich my soul.

Perseus

IT'S EASY TO HARDEN YOUR heart after you've been through the pain that leaves you questioning everything. It's easy to convince yourself that you're better off alone, that the world is safer when you're the only one in it. That's not living—that's just surviving. I'm tired of just surviving. I want to feel again. I want to believe that there are still good people out there who will see the cracks in my armor and love me not in spite of them but because of them. I want to be brave enough to let someone in, even if it means risking my heart again. I know as much as it hurts to be vulnerable, it hurts even more to live behind walls.

So, I'm slowly but surely trying to let those walls come down. I'm learning that strength isn't about shutting people out but letting them in, even when you're terrified. It's about trusting that your heart is resilient, no matter how many times it's been bruised or broken. It's about believing that you deserve love and happiness and that you deserve to be seen, heard, and held. There are days when it feels impossible when the fear of getting hurt again is almost too much to bear. Yet, to truly protect my heart is to use it, to let it be what it was meant to be: a vessel for love, compassion, and connection. It's the grace I deserve and the love I give myself.

About The Author

Erin Whitten is a writer from Massachusetts. Her work dives into human experience, capturing the beauty, messiness, and sheer irony of life's everyday moments. Whether reflecting on personal stories or societal quirks, Erin's writing invites readers to see the world a little differently, embracing both the light and the shadows we all encounter.

You can connect with her on Instagram at @erinunwritten

If you have tips for her on how to finally keep a houseplant alive—or other general inquiries—you can reach her at erinwhitten.com.

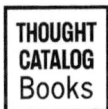

THOUGHT
CATALOG
Books

Thought Catalog Books is a publishing imprint of Thought Catalog, a digital magazine for thoughtful storytelling, and is owned and operated by The Thought & Expression Co. Inc., an independent media group based in the United States of America. Founded in 2010, we are committed to helping people become better communicators and listeners to engender a more exciting, attentive, and imaginative world. The Thought Catalog Books imprint connects Thought Catalog's digital-native roots with our love of traditional book publishing. The books we publish are designed as beloved art pieces. We publish work we love. Pioneering an author-first and holistic approach to book publishing, Thought Catalog Books has created numerous best-selling print books, audiobooks, and eBooks that are being translated in over 30 languages.

ThoughtCatalog.com | **Thoughtful Storytelling**

ShopCatalog.com | **Shop Books + Curated Products**

www.ingramcontent.com/pod-product-compliance
Lightning Source LLC
LaVergne TN
LVHW041322080426
835513LV00008B/552